ANCHOR
BOOKS

ALL THINGS PRECIOUS

Edited by

Heather Killingray

First published in Great Britain in 2003 by
ANCHOR BOOKS
Remus House,
Coltsfoot Drive,
Peterborough, PE2 9JX
Telephone (01733) 898102

SB ISBN 1 84418 270 3

FOREWORD

Anchor Books is a small press, established in 1992, with the aim of promoting readable poetry to as wide an audience as possible.

We hope to establish an outlet for writers of poetry who may have struggled to see their work in print.

The poems presented here have been selected from many entries, and as always editing proved to be a difficult task.

I trust this selection will delight and please the authors and all those who enjoy reading poetry.

Heather Killingray
Editor

CONTENTS

Altered	J P Worthy	1
An Ode For My Love	Amanda Jane Martin	2
Addendum	Robin Quarterman	3
Real, True Love . . .	Linda Roberts	4
Please Teacher	F R Smith	5
Kiss	Margarette L Damsell	6
The Writing On The Wall	Donna June Clift	7
Love *This* Century	Georgina Miller	8
Long Day Till Night	Sharon Blossom Brown	10
Nikki	Thomas Jamieson	11
So Weak	Angela Cole	12
Love Song	Jonathan Clements	13
A Poem For You	P J Littlefield	14
I'm Very Aware	R McGinty	15
Comfort	Alison Culshaw	16
Don't Be Afraid	Keith Helliwell	17
Cat Got My Tongue	John Coughlan	18
When The Time Comes	Kirsty Walters	19
Key Unto My Soul	Philip Naylor	20
Forgotten Dreams	Margaret Parnell	21
To Sleep	Neal Moss	22
Be My Valentine	Mark E Kay	23
I'm In Need Of Your Love	Mags Scorey	24
Of Course	Chris Creedon	25
Natural Disclosures	Roger Mosedale	26
Love Divine	Caroline Halliday	27
An Epitaph Of Love	D Haskett-Jones	28
Wish On A Star	Moya Muldowney	29
All Cut Up Over You	Simon McAlear	30
Till Death Do Us Part	Joyce Macdonald	31
Better Than Elves, Mr Frodo	Perry McDaid	32
Because Of You	Frank Littlewood	33
Inspiration Of Tomorrow's Eve	J Fraser	34
Ship In A Bottle . . .		
A Sailor's Lament	Martin James Banasko	35
Love . . .	Carl Thurston	36

Just Love Me Mummy	Teresa Peters	37
Midnight Wings	Josephine Easterlow	38
Don't Hurt Me Anymore	Anita Jacob	39
February Alochemy	Robert Newton	40
Poison	Karla Kerr	41
By My Side	Helen G Smith	42
Secret Love	Trevor Napper	43
Where Have You Gone?	Hilary J Cairns	44
Only A Man	Margaret Hanning	45
You're My Heart's Beautiful Vision	C R Slater	46
Insubstantial Love	Roger Penney	47
Anglers' Lodge	Kinsman Clive	48
Don't Bring Me Flowers	Gate Keeper	49
Love Is	Ian Dickson	50
The Enchantress	Vaifro Malavolta	51
It's Love	Cuthbert Makwetura	52
My First Love	Donald John Tye	53
Come In For Coffee?	Alan Chesterfield	54
My World	Kirk Antony Watson	55
Show Some Respect Sometimes To Me	Stephen A Owen	56
The Pledge	Angus Richmond	58
Lust At First Sight	Laurence DE Calvert	59
Helen	Pluto	60
Cupid's Arrow	Donna Salisbury	61
Nil Desperandum	R N Taber	62
Tweet, Tweet Love's Young Dream, Tweet Tweet	Michael D Bedford	63
Question	Mary Hughes	64
Looking My Way	Keith L Powell	65
My Angel In Disguise	Kevin McCann	66
In Tender Keeping	Anthony Rosato	67
Three Simple Words	Norman Andrew Downie	68
Cold, So Cold	Joyce Walker	69
A Crush	Ian Bowen	70
My First Love	G Jones-Croft	71
A Bowl Of Soup	G J Cayzer	72

First Love	Margaret Kaye	74
Without You	Cynthia Taylor	75
Elsker	Edward Fursdon	76
The Rose	Helen Manson	77
Just One Chaste Kiss	Stewart Gordon	78
An Awakening	Susan J Roberts	79
To Love Once Again	Phil Roberts	80
The Day	Penny Kirby	81
Woman In Love	Heather Peter	82
Red Shoes	Lola Johnson	84
Man Who Travels Alone	Chris Brownsword	86
Being In Love	Ise Obomhense	87
The Gift	Rosaline Cook	88
You	Gavin Joseph Noonan	89
The Biggest Thanks	Viv Lionel Borer	90
Bliss	Harold Wonham	91
Ups And Downs	J Gatenby	92
The Endless Road	The Warrior Poet	93
Tearing Down The Moon	Carol Wheeler	94
My Other Half	Christine Nolan	95
You	Amanda Richards	96
You	Helen Towner	97
Broken Hearted Hopes	Sarah Green	98
A Mortal Blow	Emma Jane Mountain	99
Is This Life	Marj Busy	100
A Touch Of Love	Gloria B Rogers	101
You Shattered My Dreams At Midnight	Jonathan Pegg	102
Love Lost	Ron Mayne	103
My Lover Makes Me Laugh A Lot: But In Six Inch . . .	Jackie J Docherty	104
My Love	Marie Jay	106
Don't Go	James L Wood	108
On This Her Birthday	Maddoc Martin	109
Like Torture	Lynn Thompson	110
Torn	Lyn Sandford	111
Foolish For Loving You	Jean P McGovern	112
I'm Not Ready	Annabelle Lilly	113

The Ballad Of Frenchie Le Pew	John Mitchell	114
Thinking Of You	Annette K Aiken	115
Passion Of One	C D Spooner	116
Love	Kevin McNulty	117
Let Love Guide You Through	Janice Simone Ramkissoon	118
A Life Of Love	Karen Stacey	119
The Key To My Heart	Catrina Lawrence	120
The Compliment	Gemma Davies	121
My Dream	Tonya Barber	122
The One	Colin Morrow	123
Love	Rachael Ford	124
A Dream Of Love	Maggie Hickinbotham	125
Remember	Nicky Stecker	126
Oh, My Gosh! Oh, My Gosh! Oh, My Gosh!	Denis Martindale	127
What Is Love?	Monica C Gibson	128
In Time	Natalie Ellis	129
Three Words	Andrea Benita Ross	130
Love's Fear	Heys Stuart Wolfenden	131
Mother-In-Law	Christine M Wicks	132
Just The Same Old Me	B Clark	133
Love At First Sight	D L Crichley	134
Safe In My Heart	Stephen Howsam	135
Courtship	Eleanor Dunn	136
Within	E M Gough	138
Comfort In Cotton Sheets	M M Graham	139
Tainted Love	Nicola Pitchers	140
My Heart	Sid 'de' Knees	141

ALTERED

Through that crack in a rift of time
She thought of the day she went off line
In the labyrinth of her altered mind
The right or wrong she could not define
Her reason twisted by a shadow past
From the day they met the runes were cast
She craved his touch upon her heart
Wake up with him and never part
To see him naked each new morning
Have him kiss her neck with no pre-warning
To have him sit there by her side
And not to say when she knows he lied
She wrote him letters that were never sent
Soaked by the tears she did not repent
She keeps his picture in a secret place
Yet knows his lover she will not displace
Each night she sleeps with a small blue pill
And when she wakes she will love him still
She will see him today, he lives next door
Her secret to love that little bit more.

J P Worthy

AN ODE FOR MY LOVE

Just like the wings of a bird
in a clime of motion,
do I sense my love cascade
from the skies of passion.
I feel his soft whispers
edged over me,
like a sunset in hotly flames.
He emerges before me, and from
the strings of his heart
plays the sweet music of love.
Such vibrancy he lays upon my
lips of redden deep,
beneath the moonlight of mirth.
How you move me, with silent
invitation, shimmering over
me like the kisses of rain.
We dance, and frolic aside
the flow of a gentle breeze,
as our hearts fill with joy.
Come my love, let us pledge
our love in radiant dawn,
and let it be so, that one
thousand posies shall fragrance
this love upon tendered earth.

Amanda Jane Martin

ADDENDUM

Still chasing the dead dream of my heart,
I fish for hope, of signs in your smiles,
But the sporting speech is far too busy,
Carving out the passing time.

In the yearning urgency that wastes -
Lips are callused with ghostly sense,
Until my stymied wound spoiled,
And worry grew anew on my face.

I was then for a time seized -
By the flavour of your love that wavered,
But only unrehearsed feelings remain,
Secured in the memories that linger.

Robin Quarterman

REAL, TRUE LOVE ...

We all want to be loved, cared for, appreciated,
Thinking we have found love, our hearts rule our head.
Some think it's love at a first glance,
It isn't love, it's lust or just romance.
Most of us don't know what real love is,
We think it's a feeling, or it's in a kiss,
A tingling emotion, something spoken or appearance,
Physical attraction, or passion, even romance,
We all have it mixed up, that is not real, true love . . .

Love is not what we get, it is not a feeling,
It is to do with what we give, the love we are giving.
Love is - kindness, thoughtfulness, sensitivity, total concern,
Thinking of the needs of the other person.
Love is - to be able to see
That we are making the other person happy.
Love is - not something that happens all of a sudden,
We must care for someone before we love them.
Love is - never, ever jealous.
Love comes from within us.
Romance and love go together,
We can't have one without the other.
Love grows, needs time, it has to be tested and proved
Before we know if we have a love so true.
Not many people know true love or ever find it . . .

Give love, always be friends,
Real, true love has no end,
In our world it's love we all need,
Keep on giving love and you will receive.
Reach out, give your inner self, you will find real, true love . . .

Linda Roberts

PLEASE TEACHER

Once it was said, a young man's fancy turned to thoughts of love,
But then, love was a spiritual emotion, a blessing from above,
Today . . . who needs a wedding ring or similar symbolic band?
Love is just a passing fancy - they call it a one night stand.
Once a man was captivated by the light in a woman's eyes -
She was a creature to be adored, treasured and idolised,
But enduring love is not a young man's attraction anymore,
Sex is all young people want - what teenagers are looking for,
What a shocking state of affairs this is for modern society,
We encourage our young to live a life of lust and impropriety,
Can we not teach our children the true meaning of human love -
And the ecstasy they will come to find if they really fall in love?

F R Smith

KISS

How sweet the first kiss to a newborn babe
Followed by droves in treasured wave
Until the kiss becomes a chore by Aunt
Bearing down on a child shouting, 'Shan't' . . .

But then dawns puberty, smiling or not
The stolen kiss in a parting shot . . .
What bliss becomes the teenage years
Tender . . . romantic . . . amidst all the tears . . .

So when you are married where does it go?
Out of the window with all the dough . . .

Still yet again comes a stolen kiss
A mysterious stranger (what utter bliss)
Then time to kiss the kids goodbye
'Take care, be good . . .' (try not to cry) . . .
On to kisses all round at family dos
Weddings and funerals and christening coos . . .

Then the kiss that was given so long ago
To the loved one you lived with as friend and foe
Has one final kiss at the end of their life
The kiss of death that is strident and rife . . .

Margarette L Damsell

THE WRITING ON THE WALL

In times of need, we still recall,
What we wrote on the school wall.
A love heart, initials, arrow too.
A symbol of love between we two.

Our declaration etched stone on stone,
Over the years, in depth, has grown.
But, like most, we've faced some sorrows,
Certain, together, we had no more tomorrows.

But, when out of love, we think we'll fall,
You and I will visit our garden wall.
With another heart, initials, arrow too,
Our love for each other, we do, renew.

Donna June Clift

LOVE *THIS* CENTURY

He's not my bloke ya know
We've got three kids together
So we go with the flow.
We split up a couple of years ago
I found traces of adultery
So ya know, he had to go.
A few weeks later
No, in fact it was days
I started to feel unstable
I don't know why, I bring home the bacon
And share it out on the table,
But I asked him to come back anyway
On circumstances which were understandable.
The kids of course
Without it sounding as confused as I really was
I still wanted a divorce.
It became a school play yard
After a while
Teasing increased and bullying
Didn't die down with a false smile.
And insanity rose
I know myself and this situation
So I act like this
I can't change him
He can't change me
Therefore we don't communicate through the mist.
Sometimes we'd catch it, but not for long
There was a point when our love was unbreakable
So strong
But it's definitely gone.
He goes out quite often
Probably to meet one of his 150 girlfriends
I go out sometimes, with strictly friends!

Emotions to me are like a snowball
Ready to melt, ready to fall
But something always pops up to stall.
A good job I suppose
All I ever wanted to do was make things better
And while we're playing Russian roulette
Our kids think we're together
I'm in pain
And I don't even know where he's at
When *my kids* grow up and leave
Will I laugh or cry, when I look back
The concept of love and hate
Mind boggling to work out
A perfect family portrait.

Georgina Miller

LONG DAY TILL NIGHT

Day after day
Night comes too
Loneliness sets in for you
Thinking, dreaming hoping, wishing, crying too
Solely just for special you
If only correspondence I'd get
I would be happy to spend never-ending
Undying, unbreakable, untouchable love
Spiritually given me
I want to be with you
Please hurry, contact, do something real soon
Before I explode
Wanting, needing, waiting for your call
Living in limbo is hard to do, I'm sure
Especially given the deep down
Rooted feelings beyond my or our control
Come on, share my love feelings, hope to
Put faith and trust and believe in me
'Cause what I'm saying is truly
Beyond belief
But solely true
Day 'til night
Dawn to dusk
I say how much
I love you

Sharon Blossom Brown

NIKKI

(To the best auntie in the world)

I will always love you, no matter what,
I want you to know I love you a lot.
You and your sis are the best to me,
I love you a lot as you make me feel free.

Although you are leaving, I will never forget,
Most people like you are hard to get.
When you are gone you may always return,
When I think of you my stomach churns.

I love you so much, I hope you have no fear,
That when you leave I'm gonna feel a tear.
So when you leave my heart will fall,
But I will always remember you and give you a call.

Nikki
I want you to know I will love you loads,
Love you always
Thomas xxxx

Thomas Jamieson

So Weak

I get weak
When you move your feet
I get weak
When I want to open up
When I feel alone
Feels I want to cry
I can't read your mind
But wish I could
I wonder why I sit
Sit here alone
Why am I so weak
Weak when I am not
Not with you.

Angela Cole

LOVE SONG

(For Ciara, for whenever we first met)

The smell of your skin
Lingers on my fingertips
I can taste you on my lips
As I breathe you in

I don't want to get over this
I'm choosing not to forget
Your face
Your kiss

Chorus

I don't
Want you in my memory
I want you here
(Here with me)

I'm not
Crazy to feel
Mad about missing you
You made me feel real

Chorus

I struggle
Simply to remember you
You who disappeared too soon
You're on my mind

Chorus

Jonathan Clements

A POEM FOR YOU

This is for Jan,
Simple but true,
Where would I be,
If it wasn't for you?

I'd be lost in the dark,
Stuck in the gloom,
Climbing life's staircase,
From my lonely one room.

You gave me your love,
You gave me a reason,
You are my sunshine,
No matter what season.

I worship the ground,
That you walk upon,
You are my music,
You are my song.

The years pass us by,
Our children have grown,
To make their own way,
From our nest they have flown.

Now it's just us two again,
Funny how things work out,
Together for life,
Was there ever a doubt?

So now we are old and grey,
And with life, just can't cope,
We're still filled with love for each other,
Filled with passion, ambition and hope.

P J Littlefield

I'm Very Aware

Many people are fools for Love,
But Greatest Love will keep no fools.
Most are betrayed and chained by Love,
But Greatest Love frees, soothes and cools.
Greatest Love does itself impart,
It can't be bound by earthly chains.
But lustful passion's urge would spark
The fuse of Trust's controlled restrain.
When Trust melts in another's kiss
Explosive passion feeds wild flames;
While Love's lust grabs heavenly bliss,
Greatest Love screams in hellish pain.
Then, as Greatest Love burns and dies,
Love lingers on, in Greatest Love's disguise.

R McGinty

COMFORT

garden fruits
bejewelled
by the shimmering heat

swollen raspberries plump
their ruby lips to mine
graze teeth with soft acidic spill

sweet strawberries
bear their seedy promise
to my calamitous mouth

and i would crusade their trembling
velvet kisses to your lips
and you might comfort me with apples

Alison Culshaw

DON'T BE AFRAID

If you think you should hide away
listen to what I've got to say
don't be afraid

Don't let your love disappear
even if it's love you fear
don't be afraid

One man left you crying
so you shut yourself away
but pull me in and close the door
and I'll be yours for evermore

Try and understand
my heart is in your hand
so please don't try to hide
what you feel inside
don't be afraid

Keith Helliwell

CAT GOT MY TONGUE

All those poems you wanted
All those words you asked me to write
Couldn't do it, couldn't say how I felt
Try as I might, sometimes all night
Words stuck in my throat and my head all light

Cat got my tongue, can't say how I feel
How do I convince you my love's for real?
But I've never learnt how to articulate
To express all those emotions
All those thoughts behind every caress
Doesn't mean I'm insincere
Rather be somewhere else than here
'Cause I love it, really love it, when you're near

Cat got my tongue, can't say how I feel
How do I convince you my love's for real?
I'll just have to ask, please take it on trust
All the things you'd wish I'd say
I feel them every day, every day
But every time I look at you
My one, my precious one
Cat got my tongue
Cat got my tongue
Cat got my tongue

John Coughlan

WHEN THE TIME COMES

We used to hold hands and walk down the street
We didn't envy a soul we'd meet
Where we went the sun would shine
And I'd wonder how your heart stole mine.

Things for us were never straight
But we never turned from love to hate
Obstacles littered up our path
We fought so hard to escape their wrath.

You constantly told me it'd be okay
That's what got me through the day
A smile from you would melt the ice
I always wondered why you were so nice.

But the fight against us never stopped
And my love for you was never topped
Day in, day out, we tried so hard
To be the ones to lay the cards.

Then one day you were sent away from me
The enemy wouldn't listen to my plea
Sudden they came and sudden they went
On them I could not my anger vent.

I promised you that horrible day
I would come back for you when the time came
For us to be together once more
When our love could overpower any law.

Kirsty Walters

KEY UNTO MY SOUL

My eyes, an empty sphere, to which I hold no recollection,
No swamping tears, to form a glaze of deception.
It's in my haste I speak these words of hate,
For reality beckons my views you are ornate.

Your playful soul, to which I can detest,
Your spiteful comments, I long to put to rest.
If only I could tell you of my past,
To relieve my conscious, a remedy that would last.

Inside me lies another world, so far from your perception.
It's guarded deep within my soul, to hinder interception.
Inside it lies my opposites, of which I try to hide,
But often they can overflow, like an uncontrollable tide.

Picture this, it's dark and quiet, you're paranoid with fear,
Well now it's set upon you, you know that you are near.
I long to tell you of the truth, but something tells me not to,
For this is not a tiny thing, and requires that I trust you.

Your jestful words attack my mind, I try to understand,
But when each time I reach to you, I sink beneath the sand.
You push me back, time after time, not knowing when to stop.
I hold you near unto my heart, but one day you will drop.

I'm sure there's things within my heart, to which you could relate,
But they lie hidden deep within, behind a cast iron gate.
And if you let me near enough, I'll give you then a key,
And then you'll understand it all, but you'll also understand me.

Philip Naylor

FORGOTTEN DREAMS

What happened to the dreams we shared
We built our stairway to a castle in the air
But we reached it not
That castle up there
We parted, last words unsaid
Misunderstandings can never be re-said
We had our future
Tied up in silk ribbons
But now, all is lost
Somewhere along the way
No more starlight
On our stairway to bliss
The castle crumbled
Before the last kiss
But I wish you happiness
Where ever you may be
Was it never meant to be
Just you and me?
Someone who shared
My life on the stairway
To the stars
If only we could have reached Mars

Margaret Parnell

To Sleep

Many distant hours have fled
    and minutes when our hearts have bled
Now a curtain of dark does fall
    and in my mind I hear your call

In our world I close my eyes
    seeing you my loving; prized
Through the air I sense you're near
    and wish, oh wish that you were here

Time will pass I hear you say
    to see each other another day
So rest now and be not cold
    imagine being so close to hold

Neal Moss

BE MY VALENTINE

It starts in the morning with a smile,
It means that love is here for a while.

A while can last for as long as can be,
We can make it, you will see.

Nothing beats that love for each other,
The way we really care,
Our families and friends we have around us,
That special love is rare.

They get us mad now and again,
They can be a pain,
Due to our undying love,
We manage from going insane.

Life's just happiness when you are around,
You really beat the rest,
You're one in a million and always will be
As you are the best.

The love you give, so meaningful,
In every loving way,
That's why you're so special,
Every single day.

You really are the world to me,
And everything is fine,
Would you do me the greatest pleasure,
And become my Valentine.

Mark E Kay

I'M IN NEED OF YOUR LOVE

I'm in need of your love,
like the flowers need the rain
like animals need their food,
like a cat loves its cream!

I'm need of your love,
like a mother needs her baby,
like a father needs his food!
Like a child needs loving carers.

I'm in need of your love,
like the stars need the sun,
like the sun needs the moon,
like I've never needed love before.

Mags Scorey

OF COURSE

No turtle wants to be topsy-turvy
or a giraffe tie a knot in its neck.
No model desires to be too curvy
or skipper see his ship become a wreck -
and even less do I want to lose you.

No leopard wants his spots to disappear
or the tiger lose a distinctive stripe.
No whale or dolphin wants a land-career
or diners-out wish to eat only tripe -
and even less do I want to lose you.

No one wants to follow a caravan
or a tractor in a lane going slow
Have to halt for a screeching police van
or - broken down - have to wait for a tow . . .
and even less do I want to lose you.

No hippo wants to dwell ina desert
with no river bed and no sticky mud.
No pot-bellied pig wants to wear a skirt
or city dweller have to dodge a scud . . .
and even less do I want to lose you.

No alligator yearns to have toothache.
No barn owl wants to be without a barn.
No insomniac wants to stay awake
Or audience hear the same rambling yarn . . .
and even less do I want to lose you.

No top player wants to score an own goal
No famous singer be heard out of tune
No actor wants a no talk role
Oh! You want me to *stop* this nonsense soon?
Of course . . . because I don't want to lose you!

Chris Creedon

NATURAL DISCLOSURES

Butterfly and roses,
Love adorns such poses
Of natural disclosures in flutterings of heart.

Beautiful exposures,
Eyes and lips and shoulders
Such natural disclosures sweetly taking part.

Petals gently falling,
Surrendering and falling
In natural disclosures willingly depart . . .

Till the flower is taken,
The tender root forsaken
By natural disclosures in ruthless counterpart.

Roger Mosedale

LOVE DIVINE

Kisses a treat, lips divine
When we're alone and you are all mine
I'd groan and ask for more,
Lips thicken in anticipation
Your moist tongue, takes time
Multiple orgasm, blows my mind
You don't need showing what direction
As I bring you to perfection
I whisper, 'You'll like it like this.'
The sweating and panting
The yearning for more
Shall I whisper what's in store
You know that I love you
Your lips caress mine
I love you my darling, I'm yours and you're mine.

Caroline Halliday

AN EPITAPH OF LOVE

A broken-hearted lover is sitting in his den,
In an empty house of sadness, cold and stark.
A sobbing, sighing quiver, emitting now and then,
As the whiteness of his knuckles pierce the dark.
An uncontrolled emotion is wracking in his brain,
Whilst the heaving of his body tells a tale.
The baying, swaying, crying, perpetuating pain,
Hides his nervous twitching eyelids, turning pale.

His static sitting posture convulses epic tones
And a thrashing and a throbbing fills the air.
A creaking, shrieking, cloying, pervades his helpless bones,
As an anguish and an anger meets foursquare.
His nervous disposition belies a mortal grief,
Form the thumping and a bumping in his head.
And a-twisting and a-turning in utter disbelief,
Has him yelling, a foretelling that he's dead.

The poor besotted dreamer is asking, 'Is it true?'
To the ceiling, to the walls, and to the cat.
'How can it be?' he ponders, 'I am as good as you,'
Whence collapsing in a heap, and that is that.
They found him in the morning, his eyes were staring still,
A smould'ring and a-mould'ring in the dust.
And 'neath the table written, his finger for a quill,
I love you Humpty Dumpty, fit to bust.

D Haskett-Jones

WISH ON A STAR

A single wish is all it takes,
To make a dream come true.
A single wish is all it took,
To make me fall in love with you.

I wished for someone who'd love me as I am.
Looking for beauty inside, not a pretty face.
I wished for someone who'd want to be with me always.
Everywhere I go every place.

You love me for who I am
And who I want to be.
You love me or who you see inside.
Not the outside face that everyone sees.

What we have is special.
All my love for you is returned.
Nobody could ever come between us.
No feeling will ever be spurned.

When I wished that night upon a shooting star,
A light blinded me from above.
Someone up there heard my wish
And sent me you to love.

Moya Muldowney (15)

ALL CUT UP OVER YOU

I'm all cut up over you
And now you've left me feeling blue
I didn't have a clue
But now I know it's true
I'm all cut up over you

I really need you by my side
Don't let him take you for a ride
I need to tell you how I feel
But I don't know if I can speak
Because I'm all cut up over you

Simon McAlear

TILL DEATH DO US PART

Mum said never trust a good looking man whose eyebrows meet
In the middle
Strange advice or just an old-fashioned riddle
With this in mind I just keep looking for someone I could trust
Lusting and love Mum never discussed

Dated a few lads for potential romances
Had a wee fling at the local barn dances
The good looking ones I found it hard to ignore
This eyebrow inspection soon became such a bore

I met a young chap who enjoyed a wee dram
His exuberance and wit kept me happy and calm
We drifted together and soon became a team
Sharing our lives and fulfilling our dreams

Some days when he leaves too much of a mess
With irritation and frustration I give him an appropriate address
Or if he does his own thing and takes me for granted
I fume and rave and they say I've even ranted

Then there's the close moments that only we two can share
When just being together we still know that we care
Being here for each other in any time of need
Compensates for any shortfalls of our habits in the life that we lead

As we sit in the twilight of the last fifty years
Knowing happiness hard times of blood sweat and tears
Wondering what in our lives had kept us together
Could this be a deep seated love that nothing could sever?

Joyce Macdonald

BETTER THAN ELVES, MR FRODO

One happy night I closed my eyes
to sail into a wondrous dream,
where star-blue gaze did mesmerise
and pierce my heart with sapphire beam.

I could but gape at elfin queen
whose silver smile possessed me so
and set my head to spin, careen
until my name I did not know.

Sheer waterfall of hair she wore,
reflecting hue of trees around.
In sleep I prayed my child she bore,
whose soul might thus be hale and sound.

Then I awoke and turned my head,
expecting naught but morn's chill dew,
to find two angels in my bed:
our growing child, my love, and you.

Perry McDaid

BECAUSE OF YOU

(To Ann-Maryllis, a lover's song of paradise lost)

Because of you the healing sun broke through
Dark clouds of heartache that for long had lain
Across my world: because of you the pain
Of harsh bereavement's turning screw
Began to fade, and then, because of you,
I was enriched by beauty that my eyes
Till then had never known and still defies
My power to describe. Because of you
I found I had a talent that before
Had never flowered as it did when you
In all your loveliness emerged into
My life: because of you, through the great door
Of paradise I glimpsed the joys inside.
Joys which, by your stern hand, I'm still denied.

Frank Littlewood

INSPIRATION OF TOMORROW'S EVE

As it approaches the midnight hour
I search my limited mind to scour
Words to give meaning to her
Perfection.

A timeless moment, enclosed in memory that can
Never be forgotten. Words flow beneath my thoughts as she
Fills my mind. All I can form is 'She is so beautiful.'
And this clichéd thought echoes through my
Being long after words have passed.

But I have fallen from Eden;
My Eve has led me astray by an
Apple she does not know she possesses.
She takes my heart, not knowing what it is,
But the serpent has not tempted her to try
The sweetness of knowledge,
Yet. She looks at the other fruit, tries them,
But these are not from the true tree
And so she will not understand until she realises
The truth, and meaning to her actions.

As I sit here all I can think of is
Her and the light she brings. I await
The morning, sunrise, awakening.
But as I wait I realise that all around is night;
Daylight may never come. I still wait and
Draw breath at tomorrow's Eve.

J Fraser

SHIP IN A BOTTLE . . . A SAILOR'S LAMENT

Rum, rum a bottle of rum
Pour me a drink my ship has come
Rum, rum a bottle of rum
A couple of drinks let's have some fun

Home to the wife, home to the kids
To tell them tales of the long tall ships
The lands we saw and the seas we sailed
The people we met, old friends we hailed

I'll not tell them of the seas that tossed
The swell of the oceans that we crossed
That when my mate was lost at sea
Then I died too, a part of me

It is the salt that strings my eyes
Who'd ever believe a sailor cries
So I'll only tell of a sunny clime
As I leave my sorrow in the sailor's wine

Rum, rum a bottle of rum
Pour me a drink my ship has come
Rum, rum a bottle of rum
One last drink and then . . . I'm gone . . .

Martin James Banasko

LOVE . . .

To me you are
The chiffon veil of morning mist
And every dewdrop's rainbow glist
The fragrant petals freshly kissed
By first rays of the sun's bronze disc
To me you are
Flowers unfurling to warm their midst
And the perfume that they givst
You're all the beauty of nature's gifts
Because I had noticed none of this
Until I'd first known you.

To me you are
The sultry whispering of the breeze
Softly singing through the leaves
The gentle swaying of majestic eaves
In joyful dance to Earth's melodies
To me you are
The brook that plays beneath the trees
The calmness of the mountain streams
And rivers skipping to join the seas
Because I had noticed none of these
Until I'd first known you.

Carl Thurston

JUST LOVE ME MUMMY

Little boy blue, can't tie his shoes
Do up buttons, or put on a vest
Though he tries his best
Each time he sees it as a test
Little boy blue in his own little world
Would rather watch telly, then read a book.
He'd rather play with Lego, than try to pull up a sock
He'd rather cuddle, than learn his ABC or 123
Little boy blue tries to play
But the other children want him to go away
He doesn't fit in with all the rest
Although he tries his best
Little boy blue, tries to tell you what he has done
But if it seems like no one's listening, it's not much fun
Mummy! Mummy! Look what I have done
Three steps with Lego bricks, oh wow what fun!
Praise and applause are what I need to hear
And it's nice when you shed a tear
For something I have achieved
It's taken me forever
To finally draw you that little flower
It maybe not look like much, but I have done my best
Just love me Mummy and I will do the rest
Well done, well done are words I need to hear
We can get through this Mummy
Just love me, cuddle me, praise me
Together we can do it
Together we can pass this test
But most importantly
Just love me Mummy and I will do the rest!

Teresa Peters

MIDNIGHT WINGS

I never seem to understand or ask the reason why,
'Cause when I feel my midnight wings I just gotta fly
Out into the fragrant air, the magic's here it seems,
Cruising down the highway of all my hopes and dreams.
The moon's a ghostly shadow such a brilliant sight,
I'm glad I found my midnight wings on this Valentine's night.
I know not where I'm going nor where I'm coming from
But I can hear the lyrics drifting from our favourite song
The music wraps around me as it floats into the air,
It was then that I first saw you . . . standing waiting there.
I saw the smile upon your face as I began to glide,
Just then I noticed someone else was standing by your side,
You didn't even see me as I soared above your head,
You looked into her eyes and gave her a rose of red
I hovered there in silence, in a trance and in despair
I reach out for a one time love to find he wasn't there.

Josephine Easterlow

DON'T HURT ME ANYMORE

Can't take the pain of loving you
When you're no longer there
And have someone new

You've given yourself
To someone else out there
Now my heart is crying
And you really don't care

I was there for you
When you needed me
I thought you had some feelings
How wrong could I be

Thrown aside like a
Child does a toy
In the same way to me
You've managed to destroy

I hope my tears will
Stop one day
And my feelings for you
Will eventually fray

I'll realise you weren't
Really good for me
And then how lucky
I shall be when
My eyes eventually see.

Anita Jacob

FEBRUARY ALCHEMY

It didn't happen often in that room
Behind the narrow door beneath the eaves.
A dawning sun dispelled the February gloom
And warmed our waking by a few degrees.
The cottage window focused sunlight in
Across you as you looked out that day's clothes,
Enriching the pale velvet of your skin;
Ennobling every pause into a pose.
It danced like diamonds in your tumbled hair
And flashed with silver from your darkened eyes.
It lingered down each sensuous line, and where
Your curves and contours filled, it alchemised
You into Grecian beauty - out of time:
Out of the morning rush, into my rhyme.

Robert Newton

POISON

A circle snared into a square,
Knife I sharpened that left me bare,
You gave me shelter from the rain,
In your fist you had the pain,
For my eyes you were the way,
I was the work; you were the play,
When the fog began to lift,
I realised your true gift,
Had not abandoned just replaced,
The lethal poison that was laced,
In a puzzle buried in the maze,
Where the nightmares come to graze,
Underfoot and hooves of thunder,
Blinded eyes look on in wonder,
Deafened to the merry tune,
Banished sun and worshipped moon,
In the hidden crawled to hide,
Survival pushed all else aside.

Karla Kerr

BY MY SIDE

I saw the hills, the trees and the wood,
Their beauty was great, and I cried,
I wanted to share the sight, so good,
I wanted you there by my side.

I walked through the garden of roses sweet,
In my mind, perfumes lingered inside,
The faces of daisies and poppies did greet,
I wished you were there by my side.

I stepped on the moss and the grass with its dew,
The myriad flowers couldn't hide
Their radiance, their petals with delicate hue,
I hoped you'd be there by my side.

I thought of the morning, the freshness of dawn,
The fulfilment of day not denied,
The birds of the air, butterflies on the lawn,
I prayed you'd be there by my side.

I heard the ripple of water in streams,
By the sea, watched the rise of the tide
And sailed far away in a ship in my dreams,
I felt you were there by my side.

I reflected on times past and mountains I'd climbed,
Different paths and routes that I'd tried
And when I had stumbled, your help was well timed . . .
I knew you had been by my side.

Helen G Smith

SECRET LOVE

For many years come what may,
Few can ignore St Valentine's Day.
Although one person who lowered the tone,
Was a gentleman known as Al Capone.

You can ask someone to love you,
All of your life.
But add the proviso,
Don't tell the wife.

A man may have a crush on a woman,
Or a woman on a bloke.
Is it all serious
Or is it a joke?

Anyone can be a Valentine,
The choice is free.
Once I sent a special one,
Addressed to *me.*

Trevor Napper

WHERE HAVE YOU GONE?

Where have you gone, for all I see
Are shreds of what you used to be,
A look I do not recognise,
A distant blankness in your eyes
That once met mine in harmony.

Dispassionate facsimile,
You dwell a million miles from me,
A stranger in a well known guise,
Where have you gone?

Your eerie shade has broken free
From our exquisite unity;
You took your leave with no goodbyes,
Forsaking me by your demise,
Bequeathing me your memory,
Where have you gone?

Hilary J Cairns

ONLY A MAN

For the large silly coward you turned out to be
for the weakness and vast immaturity
for your lack of loyalty your failure to fight
knowing it's wrong but too sick to put right.
for the feelings you lost when things suddenly twisted
Your failings I find are too long to be listed!
You run fast from trouble
it's then you don't care
for the love, warmth and longing
you said *once* were there.
From facing the facts you beat fast retreat
not caring for others who fall at your feet
you blatantly flaunt but still will not say
that you're 'sorry' - 'forgive me', before going away.
no - you are a *man*, no more than a name
and basically I find you're all just the same,
you chase want and love one
but when trouble comes
you're the first to take cover
or turn tail and run.
How fast love's forgotten and dreams pushed aside
the ache deep inside and the tears one has cried,
so wasted I find, yet I know that I can
forget once again -
you are *only* a *man!*

Margaret Hanning

YOU'RE MY HEART'S BEAUTIFUL VISION

Your eyes of blue, they melt my heart,
When I hold your hand, nothing could part,
When we two kiss, you can almost hear a hiss,
Of the heated desire, that sets us afire.
I love your face, I know its every little trace
I desire your body; in such perfect place.
You are my one and only dream come true,
And my knees go weak, when I am with you.
You are the angel in my dreams each night,
A vision of beauty, with love shining bright,
You are the stars that twinkle up high,
Being with you makes me feel I could fly.
You have an incredible, truly awesome, sweet smile,
That makes me forget this is real, for a while.
I could write about you, on and on forever
And the ending would always, be simply, never.
You see, my love is eternal, only for you
And like a swan, never-ending, real and so true.

C R Slater

INSUBSTANTIAL LOVE

Love, as insubstantial as a cloud.
Or as the mist on Scottish mounts,
Hangs wreathed around the crags.
Then as quickly drifts away, or
Evaporates in air, thin, dreamlike,
Ghostly and unreal.
Yet love, as real, as capable,
Of letting in the sun and light
Of day. Of drying out the chill,
Of loneliness, and of giving substance,
To longings unexpressed, or,
Inexpressible in words. Words,
Clumsy, heavy-booted and,
Foolishly crude for such a task.
But love, as light of day.
To sweet enchanted minds.
Not moonstruck, maudlin nor,
Unsound, where dampness lurks,
Undermining foundations hard.
But shadows; all driven off,
By heat and light and warmth.
And love as real as loving.
Confirmed to heart and mind.

Roger Penney

Anglers' Lodge

November!
Closed season.

Clear morning.
Brilliant sun.
Every blade of grass
is weighed down with
frost's sparkling armour.

A stillness came
with the morning's wake.
Although everything is sharp,
the countryside,
lies sleeping.

She . . . *beautiful creature,*
is leaning on the veranda rail.
Captivated . . .
by the lakeside scene.
He . . .
watches and waits . . .
for her inviting smile . . .

Dull November?

Kinsman Clive

DON'T BRING ME FLOWERS

Don't bring me flowers
They say too much
Don't hold my hand
I don't like your touch
Don't say you love me
For I don't care
Don't say I love you
For I am unaware
Don't say you need me
For I don't need you
Don't say you're faithful
For I am untrue
Don't grieve at my going
I'll not grieve too much
Don't long to be near
You don't mean that much.

Gate Keeper

LOVE IS

Love is like a shadow, it's meant to be,
love is a leaf which clings to its tree,
love is a blossom of sweet white wine,
love is a sparkle which needs to shine,
love is you and you are mine,
love is a light suspended in time,
love is true, love is faith,
love is two shadows walking in line,
love is what love is and that is what we are
it isn't something we can see,
it's like a rainbow which goes on forever
or like a fire that never dies.
Happiness and love is in our eyes
it is something we are.

Ian Dickson

THE ENCHANTRESS

Shall I compare you
To a summer's night
Filled with mysterious lights
Warm and exciting,
Or to a summer's field
Luscious grass. Myriad of flowers
Beautiful, wild and . . . intoxicating?
Yet, I will compare you to a rose
Queen of the flowers' kingdom. Alas!
Like you, roses too have thorns.
Casual, empty words of mine . . .

As I stand all wrapped up
Lost in deep thoughts
My inner-self quivers
In dread anticipation.
To be near . . . !
Hold you, just one more time.
To feel the warmth, the softness
Of your tumid breasts. The delight
Of a sweet caress. And,
Drag myself deep, deep down
Into your loveliness . . . !

Vaifro Malavolta

IT'S LOVE

When it grips them
Reason escapes and instinct dominates
It all feels childish and foolish
It's love.

Be cunning, be clever, be a murderer
When stroked with fingers of love
You are reduced to a humble animal
Without brain without cunning powers
It's love.

Get into pillow talks
They build castles in the air
Solve all problems all at once
Travel the whole world
Fulfil things beyond their riches
He is bankrupt but talks about
Buying a yacht and a villa
It's love.

When it comes to lovemaking
Kids are chased out
Doors slammed and locked
Windows closed
Curtains drawn in
Lights turned off
It's love.

Cuthbert Makwetura

MY FIRST LOVE

My first love was an angel
No longer by my side
Her name was Gillian Rose Gwinnette
And she made a beautiful bride
Her love was so warm and tender
Her love was so soft but strong
And I just wish that I
Could have held and loved her
For my whole life long

But one day she said goodbye
Which broke my heart and made me cry
And so now I sit all alone
With my life so empty
And a heart as heavy as a stone
Just wondering where my first love
Has now gone

Donald John Tye

COME IN FOR COFFEE?

It's only instant: this attraction,
a heartbeat turn of head or hand
that floats the mind, a flash, a fantasy
that winks where glances calculate; frailties,
dark roots, the cicatrix that curls the lip
stillborn.

Alan Chesterfield

My World

Whatever yesterday felt like
to us, virtually dismiss it.
And although the hurt is
invisible. It is there.
There's no sunshine left
for me and you. I can't
endanger myself now.
It may last forever.

The reason is your love
is gone. It's brought
stormy weather into
my world.

I've done the best I can.
That's what I accept
when I try to deal with
everything. I won't
be able to grow if you
persist.

Kirk Antony Watson

SHOW SOME RESPECT SOMETIMES TO ME

I picked you up from work
you had an early shift
I got up with you
yes, getting up that early, it hurt
Two in the morning is not a good time
to drive to the city, no it's not a crime
but I took you there and I picked you up
no thanks from you
just a grumpy look

show some respect sometimes to me
'cos I don't deserve all this frustration you take out on me
tell me you need me
tell me you care
and let's leave the bad temper
and the moody stare at work
I do all I can for you and even that bit more
so treat me the way I treat you or I'll show you the door

right now it's me who does not work
but that don't make you any better
that should make you care
when I was working and you were in my shoes
I tried to cheer you up
I never gave you the blues
so just think for a minute, just think what you say
or soon I will leave you, yes I will go away
if you feel you are at the end, if you feel you cannot give no more
then let me know in a kind way and don't pretend no more

this is about respect
that's all this is about
I don't wanna lose it with you and believe me
I don't wanna shout
but I deserve better from you, I deserve a great deal more
I don't want to feel like s**t I don't wanna feel it no more . . .

Stephen A Owen

THE PLEDGE

Forever we did love
in love's open sea
Forever loving
he loved only me
Forever wife
as happy as happy can
Women are rightly jealous
of my man

A long time we loved
for all men to see
Our love was without stain
for him and me
We pledged our vows
upon a certain day
Nothing can sweep
its memory away

You loved me dear husband
to a degree
I loved you my dear
like a decree
A good wife stands
behind a loving man
Rejoice with me ye women
if you can

Angus Richmond

LUST AT FIRST SIGHT

Every time they meet
fast-moving looks are exchanged;
each time they reach an immaculate
climax without even touching
standing in the queue at the post office;
He's old enough to be her father
if he were a pop star,
he would appear thirty years younger,
She's old enough to be his mistress;
a rebel-child; no underwear and a warm heart;
an image born out of sadness and solitude;
then back they go to different locations
and once again their minds can explore;
touch and feel
making all the moves their exteriors
would never consummate in daylight hours.

Laurence DE Calvert

HELEN

If ever I should love again years away from now
I should look into two blue eyes and compare them once again to yours
To look past, further past the Elysian field where there's no
                                           looking back
Maybe as Helen with Troy not quite deceived and yet as Paris leaves:

To look once more at this citadel where the wraths of passion seed
Intangible bricks of batteries a victory to exceed

The candidate to look for as professional must not act to excess
With rapturous looks, sighs and groans perfection to extract
The selected intellectual will know the sequestered treat
Not to mimic once again that first and last defeat.

Pluto

CUPID'S ARROW

This love is magic,
It's never out of fashion.
I'm spellbound by your charms.
I have found an everlasting love,
Within your loving arms.

'Twas Cupid with his golden wings,
That brought us close together,
A clever man, who knew his stuff,
Made a love that will last forever.

You are the one that makes me whole,
You are in my heart and mind,
You know my secret soul.

Many chapters my life has had,
A vast volume of stories to tell.
But the moment that I saw you,
I fell under Cupid's spell.

Donna Salisbury

Nil Desperandum

I sought you in summer sunshine,
among autumn leaves, in winter snow;
I found you one springtime
but had to let you go - because
the world was turning too fast
and I lost my balance;
I'll seek again in summer rain,
weepy autumns, winter's passion
for despair, chance that fortune cease
its creaking wheel at such a spot
where, even yet, festering wounds
might heal though worldly rot congeal;
Fool, among other names,
I hear hypocrites accuse;
More to life than games
of hide-and-seek . . .

True. Even so, no fate worse
than giving up on us

R N Taber

TWEET, TWEET LOVE'S YOUNG DREAM, TWEET TWEET

A mortal blow was struck
By Cupid's little arrow
She, thin, tall and tanned
Mouth open but no speech
But when she turned away
On one knee I preached
When I heard a yes
Ding dong the bells did ring

So for rest of day
All I did was sing

Michael D Bedford

QUESTION

Blankness in my mind,
Coldness across the earth,
Soundless the music's voice,
Gone life's worth.
Where can the answer be?
Shattered the hopes,
Reality gives the lie,
To words we spoke.
All of the time passing,
Now quite apart,
What can I tell,
My restless heart?

Mary Hughes

LOOKING MY WAY

You said that she was looking my way
You said that she could not think of anything to say
Think of anything to say oh
Think of anything to say.

You said that she wanted to come over my way
But she could not think of anything to say
Think of anything to say oh
Think of anything to say.

You said that she felt like crying all the way home
Because she could see herself forever being on her own
Being on her own yes
Being on her own.

Keith L Powell

MY ANGEL IN DISGUISE

She has been a guiding influence,
over these last few years -
  And she's been known to just be there,
especially when one's about to shed some tears.
  By her very presence
and her matron-like air -
  She leads others by example,
and in showing that she does really care.
  During an errand or that message,
she will always find some time -
  To be of some help and comfort,
to others, especially this one penning this lyrical rhyme.
  From her cordial, bedside manner,
to the sincerity of those eyes -
  She means so much to me,
she's become my angel in disguise.
  Just as in those times before,
and by the things she's had to do -
  She has always proved her capability,
in coping with folks like me and you.
  There's a message in this poem,
so poignant, and yet so true -
  To this particular angel in disguise,
I now want to dedicate this piece to you.

Kevin McCann

IN TENDER KEEPING
(Dedicated to Caroline)

If culture could keep a friend without fear,
Who knows now where we would be.
The fortunes of life may meet us in soul
And the sights within our eyes could then see.
No blindness, no kinder, no emptiness or chose
Just a blessing, with love
And a dew-moist wet rose
With the eighth a beginning, than an end as it was
I would take you as feelings may grow in their care
What al over you'd be and a woman to share;
To tickle and tease, pamper and light
With a taste of your honey to reach you in height
Your breasts full-born, to be suckled in prize,
Your lips forever moistened, so deep in their hedge
The power of love could insert its deep wedge:
And the mesh of eternity may choose by its stars
I would want you as my Venus, not as my Pluto or Mars.

Anthony Rosato

THREE SIMPLE WORDS

I love you those soft lips did say.
What joy and happiness they did bring.
Not knowing soon my dreams were to be shattered.
Sadness and gloom to take their place.

Now I sit and wonder why.
My heart you have broken.

Did I reach for a twinkling star too far
Or has someone taken my place?

I hope he never hurts you and treats you right.
For you my lovely deserve the best and love in your life.

May I say those three simple words

I love you

Will stay in my heart forever

Norman Andrew Downie

COLD, SO COLD

Cold, so cold
The winter of my discontent.
My body numb
Was once so summer warm
When love begun.

Cold, so cold
The winter of my discontent
You came and made me sing.
Then took away from me all feeling
When you went.

Joyce Walker

A CRUSH

Finally when I
Had left the Navy
I searched for a girl
Who could make good gravy
I did not care
If she was fat or thin
As long as she put
Lots of Oxos in.

Then I found a girl
Good with the sauce
For forty years now
We've got the course
So I must have chosen
From the right stock
As she still crushes and mixes
Shaking her wok.

Ian Bowen

MY FIRST LOVE

I saw your face,
I loved you then.
If I was to see your face
Again,
I would love you
Now.

G Jones-Croft

A BOWL OF SOUP

Today's recipe: My love, as it was for you. A gentle and
delicate, precious thing.

Ingredients: Take two people any age or gender. (So long
as their hearts be true.)
Rich . . . poor. In good health or in pain.
Colour . . . creed, read and accept, as
mentioned above, for gender.

Preparation: Combine the two ingredients (ie you and I).
Go to a special place, secret if preferred.
Allow generous amounts of time for talking
walking, as required. Another method, often
used, learn to blend and be as one, eg to sit,
hold hands. To be consumed with a feeling,
never truly felt before. (was it the same
sensation you had, as the one I felt for you.)

Cooking Time: The burning heat of wild passion,
erm possibly. Good, if you want your recipe
to be done quickly. For others, a slow and
steady heat. Broad even flames to go
all around. Nothing missed, over cooked . . .
or underdone. Just right.

Serving Suggestion: Place on a table with ample room. Nothing
to be squashed or jammed in. This needs
room to breathe. Serve up as large a portion
as you feel able enough to eat. Savour the
taste. Consume every mouthful . . . from the
first to last. Wipe your bowl clean. Should
you wish to partake of more, do so. One can
never have enough of something as good as
this.

Comments: Remember this for what it was and what you had. For this is the magic, that all true lovers have. Without it . . . lose it, your life would be very sad.

G J Cayzer

FIRST LOVE

Such sad and bitter tears are shed
at that aching first lost love

They fall upon hardened ground . . .
Laying there in pools of
grey and fetish water
In unrelenting acid soil . . .
Until the warm winds and dry air
come to soak them up . . . but . . .
They leave behind
Indentations which are so hard
to ever level again

If only it was known before . . .
They can . . . and they do

Margaret Kaye

WITHOUT YOU

Nothing rhymes without You,
Without You, Jesus nothing rhymes,
The clock goes tock tick,
And the blackbird's now a peculiar shade of blue
Without You, Jesus without You.
Without You, the apple's square.
The stars shine out at noon.
Without You, without You.
Without You - there is no reason and there is no time
And time itself, becomes a void, without You, without You, Jesus
Without You, the sparrow's song is muted when it's dawn.
The frog no longer spins her skein of spawn.
Creation's throbbing heart is torn
And life itself becomes a pawn.
Without You - without You - Jesus - without You.

Cynthia Taylor

ELSKER

Was it love
when first you looked at me
above the cocktail throng;
was it love
that made us meet again
although it seemed so wrong -
was it . . . love?

Was it love
to feel your tousled hair
a cushion for my eyes;
was it love
to see yours open wide
in wondering surprise -
was it . . . love?

Was it love
the soft blue-veined marble
proffered – flawless, white;
was it love
your drowning kisses in
the oceans of the night -
was it love?

Was it love
all too intense to bear
that fused your heart to stone -
your chilling cold which numbed
all being, and left me
deadened and alone;
was it . . . my love?

Edward Fursdon

THE ROSE

As we walk through the garden in love the lilacs bloom
up above, I take your hand so white as a dove and I
place it on my gentle breast as I pick a red rose
for your dress. Where there is love the heart is light.
Where there is love the day is bright. Where there is
love there is a song, and I shall sing it all life long.
I have got a red, red rose it always blooms in spring
it is a symbol of my love it is a bonnie thing I shall keep
my red, red, rose until I find my queen, when I have I shall
love her dearly till the last rose blooms (forever) love
is a gift that was sent by God for all of us to share it
was sent by a little flower and nothing can compare.
It is a bonnie red, red rose I'll give it to my queen
And she shall keep it till all the petals fall.

Helen Manson

JUST ONE CHASTE KISS

Just one chaste kiss,
Is all I ask and place your hand in mine
And walk with me a little while
Along the sands of time.
Besides the murmuring sea,
A soft caressing breeze,
A silver moon shines in the sky
And puts us at our ease.
No one need know the bliss we've shared
In that most hallowed land,
No trace is left in time or mind
For anyone to find.
Just one chaste kiss,
Your hand in mine
And footprints in the sands of time.

Stewart Gordon

AN AWAKENING

I kissed your rosy lips
and I knew peace no more.
My feelings a turmoil
of desire and ecstasy,
soaring to unknown heights
and I was lost!

I am yours forever
You made me see my reality
helped me overcome
my fears and frustrations,
my doubts and desperation.
I kissed your lips
and I was born again.

Susan J Roberts

To Love Once Again

And then . . . when suffering love . . . yields too cruel hate
Every invisible burden carried as a cross . . . mocks
Magnified, the heavy shackles
Gluing you together appear boulder size
And the hope of recuperating loneliness
Seems an impossible dream

The painful break finally reveals the desire
You cherish the time to breathe in new life
And new experiences
The lightness you now feel is heavy with memories
Experienced memories, not to take you back,
But to guide and show a brighter way
As hurt and hate dispel, you heal . . . and you're ready . . . once again

Phil Roberts

THE DAY

My dream came true
The day I was
Blessed with you
Your loving eyes
Met mine and smiled
You hold me close
Whispering my name
My heart melts and sighs
A dream came true
The day I
Was blessed with you.

Penny Kirby

WOMAN IN LOVE

Pou la premier fois je pense
Jai le Coeur brise
It is like an electric fire that rages.
It rages with an intensity that
Consumes my inner being
Mon cheri, pour quo?

Your venom is like that of a cobra
Lethal.
Such a player
Your charm. Your adoration. Your devotion.
All but a game to you.
How much I would love to hate you.
You do know that don't you?

The anguish. The mortification. The bitterness.
All of what you caused.
Because of this suffering
I am now enclosed in a cocoon.
C'etait fatal.
Le sias que.

Oh! La! La! La passion.
I could still recall your words of comfort that night
When you held me,
When you touched me,
Saying that everything was going to be ok
After a night of intense lovemaking.

Back then; I believed your every word
Fulfilled your every desire
Your every wish
Your every command.
Little did I know

I would be in this room.
The institution
For the unbalanced ones, they said.
But I am not unbalanced I say,
I am in love.

Heather Peter

RED SHOES

I had a dream last night
Of red shoes and soft glowing lights
Swaying of hips, a soft guitar sound
The distant sound of beating waves
And smell of the salty air and the deep sea
Laughter and murmurs on a small Atlantic beach
A warm night, clusters of people everywhere

I dreamt of music, strumming of chord after chord
Me, tapping my feet in my glistening red shoes
Wanting to dance but feeling shy
The hue of nightfall, a slight red streak in the sky
Fireflies hovering above, giving a golden light
Warm sand running through my fingers
Feeling the warm breeze stroking my skin

I dreamt of you, you gazing at me
Me, looking down at my red shoes
Wondering what you were thinking
Your eyes hidden by the night lights
Trees nearby, standing like hovering angels
Me, looking up to see the ethereal glow in the dark sky
Wanting to hold your hand, the hand on the guitar

I dreamt of happiness, in the shape of a dance
Me, dancing on the edge of the beach
Red shoes immersed in golden sand
Laughing, clicking my heels and twirling around
You, eyes twinkling, fingers strumming fast
A melodic tune dancing on the waves
Waves collapsing on the edge of the beach in laughter

I had a dream last night
Of red shoes floating on blue ocean waters
Me, eyes searching, standing at the edge of the sea,
Forlorn, naked toes plunging into sinking sand
Lingering, straining my ears for just one more melody
Waves lapping gently at my feet, ocean composed,
The words of a song echoing through my head

Lola Johnson

MAN WHO TRAVELS ALONE

Sat beneath a bridge
watching murky water
roll on by.
A swallow darts
amongst the trees,
it holds visions
to be shared by no other,
its wings have scraped
the floors of Heaven,
a song of jubilee
falls from its beak.
I walk alone amongst factory sprawl,
a lonesome skip in an abandoned lot
houses only plastic sheets and the
broken bottles of Friday night.
I rest in tawny overgrowth
and watch clouds creep like moss
over the great above
as the lonesome swallow lands
on a rusty pushbike
laying dead and lifeless next to
a derelict heroin syringe,
De Montherlant wrote
'The man who travels alone is a devil'
as I sip sour-love fragments
of my broken heart
from a chipped shot glass
forged in the fires of Hell.

Chris Brownsword

BEING IN LOVE

I get butterflies in my stomach
and get excited whenever you're around.
We stare into each other's eyes without saying a word.
Letting our eyes do all the talking for us.

Ise Obomhense

THE GIFT

Love, it is a baffling thing
not all who seek will find.
It sees imperfect people perfectly
I thank you for teaching me
this gift passed on in time.

And life is never perfect
some dreams they may fall through
but knowing what you have in love
every day life is brand new.

When life can seem unfair
and difficult to cope
many miss the silver lining
because they expected gold.

And when you start to lose your faith
just look around the room
each miracle in families face
was all inspired by you.

Life has many lessons
some of which are hard
but each of them make us human
and teach us all to love.

The lessons you have taught me
are all special in my heart
you graced me with your rarities
which make me strong and proud.

There aren't adequate words to write
or sounds to string along
that could tell you what you mean to me
or how unique you really are.

Rosalind Cook

You

On this night, I will stretch my soul by our candlelight,
in shadows a'dance.
On this spring of delight, I will come to your heart, share the moon
grace; twinkling stars winking.
As met that day, my step to you will be kindled by all that I can be;
for you, ego less wishes.
One truce, made the same time that our loving met; passion of
each heart; no more, no more.

Not keeping up my love, nor you or me, but to walk the hills side
by side, till natural partings come.
Birds a flight, watch their glory, as when nature beckons they flay not
but hold to the winds; to wings a place.
And my hands hold you with what can only be echoed for my spirit and
no other; not with your grace love, your eyes are my fuel, up
to nature's cry.

And my flesh permits less than one's need; to be you, to feel your
moments, your grazes, to know your dreams, not in words,
but in them as though my own. Not to meet you that half distance
but to take it all, to become you, to have you entire, this night,
this flame of passion, this truth. How else am I to stretch my soul,
sweet love? How else am I to know you to my 'will's' desire?

My strife is my love for you; in losing myself in the game we play,
to hold the heat forever between us, to make what is sparse universal.
My time is in nature's call, nature's cry, but my sweet,
when that day comes when we fly away to our places given to us,
I can say that I was with you, that my half was met, that my life was
made, all in your sweet embrace.

Gavin Joseph Noonan

THE BIGGEST THANKS

Love in the air, once there to be, love in the air, gone like a bee.
Born to love and hurt - which one will love . . .
Which one will hurt, which one to heal -
Which one will inflict, which one's which!

You said you loved me, once said to be,
You said you hated me, just like I'd see.
Both think the same, feel the same.
Hurt the same, inflict the same - which one's which!

Together forever that's what you said,
Never together laid on my head.
Which one will be loved, which one will be lovely?
Which one will be happy, which one will be sad - which one's which?

The moon shone on my bed, at night,
You tore us apart by daylight.
Both will die -
One will be remembered?
One will be forgotten? - Which one's which!

Don't know what to do about you,
I'm confused, forgotten, thanks to you.
Two hearts, gone where?

Stolen moments . . .
It is time for loving . .
Giving and sharing,
This is how I feel.
With the man who is caring,
The moments are so special,
When we are together,
I wish that we could always - stay together . . .
Together . . . together what do you think?

Viv Lionel Borer

BLISS

'To kiss is bliss.'
So what's amiss?
Familiar this,
To kiss like sis -
No joy, no bliss.

But he's in Diss
And you're in Liss
So where's the risk?
Come, cross the abyss.
A stolen kiss
Like this and this
And this and this
and thisthisthis -
Now all's amiss:
To kiss is bliss!

Harold Wonham

Ups And Downs

See saw
You with someone new
See saw
You gazing into her eyes
See saw
You smiled your dazzling smile
See saw
You weren't mine anymore.

J Gatenby

THE ENDLESS ROAD

When all the roads seem endless,
Try not to feel despair,
For at the end of each of our roads,
Someone will be there,
Someone to call a friend,
If you believe in me he said,
I'll be there at your end.

In the evening of your life my friend,
I'll be close to you,
Ready to help and carry your load
And to see you come on through,
So when the road seems to be endless,
Look!
And I'll be there,
To help you through and overcome
And take you from despair

The Warrior Poet

TEARING DOWN THE MOON

How do I dismantle the stars
From the night you gave me the sky
How can I go back down this path
You so happily led me this way

Tell me how I can tear down the moon
And return to nights cold and black
What do I do with these days full of hours
That used to be spent with you

How can I ever erase all the words
You whispered and scarred in my head
And the memory of your smile you now
Give to someone else instead

Carol Wheeler

MY OTHER HALF

My husband is my one true love,
My soul mate and my friend,
We'll never part, our lives we'll share,
Together, to the end,
My life it has no meaning,
Unless you're by my side,
I need you to be strong and true,
Your strength to be my guide,
You're always in my thoughts,
Come night, come day,
I can't imagine life without you,
Please don't ever stray.

Christine Nolan

YOU

V . . .
Can I have a moment to dream,
to consider the possibility, you?
Can I have a second to breathe,
inhale the very thought of you?
Can I have the right to imagine,
to feel the presence that's you?
Can I openly confess to the idea,
the notion of you?

Can I play these whims thus,
the silence, the knowing of you?
Can I have just one glance now
to experience the touchable you?
Can I carry this dream on,
even without you?
Can I keep the treasure of nearly?
A secret of minds, me and you . . .
M

Amanda Richards

YOU

The chemistry between us is magic
I felt it through your heart
The night I lay in your arms
Wishing we would never part.
Maybe it was just lust?
My heart missing a beat
When I said goodbye that morning
You just fell back to sleep.
I really want to meet you again
But your feelings were not made clear
I wait until we meet again
But it's the rejection that I fear.

Helen Towner

BROKEN HEARTED HOPES

I see you my knees still go weak
I hear you and my heart skips a beat
As you talk I long for you to kiss my lips
To hold me in your arms whilst I feel your heartbeat in your chest
To hear you whisper you love me in my ear
To feel your fingers running through my hair
Oh how I wish that you were still here
What I would give and what I would sell
Just to have you near me once again.

Sarah Green

A MORTAL BLOW

My heart's a prison
you're all I know
falling for you. Again
an arrow
pierced my heart.
Lethal
not knowing
if I'll recover.

Cupid's blazing arrow
sharp, distructive
it got me
not wanting the
hurt, the pain,
and the heartache.

Then
you looked at me
your false smile,
I knew
my heart assumed it.

Our private language
distorted, burnt, lost.
that last kiss
destructive on its own
an everlasting stain
a mortal blow.

Emma Jane Mountain (16)

IS THIS LIFE

Passionate embraces
Erotic moments
Bodies entwining
Fascinating delights.
All over the world
In so many places,
These moments happen.
And that explains
Why nine months later
A child is born,
Is this why
The world was created?

Marj Busy

A TOUCH OF LOVE

Longing to be near you
Never to let go
Running fast to bring you back
Loving you - loving you so
Touching you all over
Holding you close to my heart
Knowing that I love you
Never again to part
Feeling warm all over
Just because you're near
Whispering I love you
Whispering in your ear
To live my life without you
Would be a living death
There is no life without you
And yet - and yet
I felt a chill run through me
A silent falling tear
I reached out to touch you
But nobody was there.

Gloria B Rogers

YOU SHATTERED MY DREAMS AT MIDNIGHT

Like a pebble thrown into a placid pool,
You shattered my dreams on the midnight hour.
You scattered my dreams
And cast them uncaring to the ground,
I shed my tears long after midnight,
After you had telephoned to tell me,
You were never going to return.
And during the hours of darkness,
I cried myself bone dry.
Wondering why you left my heart to die.
Come the daybreak, I see the dawn no more,
Me, lying awake, spying those distant stars,
Which I had once considered ours.
Now all I see is endless darkness,
Spilling with ice-crystal showers.
Tonight I see nowhere there's the moon,
This brief night in balmy June,
Became an endless night in chill December.
Remembering our love to be going, going, gone.
You were the one I'd vowed to love eternally,
I had seen you always as my perfect angel.
Now in my quiet desperation
See you only as a dispassionate stranger,
Left me like the unmasked, Lone Ranger.
My amigo, dear brave Tonto, riding on
Into last evening's flaming setting sun.
Seems no power on Earth would stop you.
The sunrise sees my prone and lonely body,
With an empty barbitone bottle besides me.
Now cold and lifeless on the bedroom floor.

Jonathan Pegg

LOVE LOST

I saw a sign-post
In your face

Leaning - bent, twisted
To some other place

Ron Mayne

MY LOVER MAKES ME LAUGH A LOT:
BUT IN SIX INCH STILETTOS LIFE'S JUST TOO HOT!

Well I've had all sorts of boyfriends, of all shapes and guises,
And believe me some of them in the hunk stakes would win first prizes!
But sadly I've found that the best men around who'll sweep me off
the ground, are those that come in small sizes.
For as long as they have the gift of nice chat, and are good at doing that,
then for me as a warm girly, they're never too early and give me plenty
of time with lots of hurly burly.
My latest Prince Charming, whom I really love well;
Does everything right and likes me to sing like a ding, dong bell.
There's just one thing that I'm not quite sure of though,
Even though he's the most likeable and loveable, so and so.
He likes me to wear six inch stilettos all day and night!
This fetish for my feet is nice, he likes me to rise to a great height!
But at the end of the day, it's not all that romantic in six inch heels,
I want to please him and I know that he makes me laugh and
I know how he feels.
I try to hide the fact that my plates of meat can't stand too much heat;
And though I giggle and laugh, nothing can help my poor aching feet.
I don't mind wearing those slinky and tight lurex bum-clinging thongs,
And he paid for a tattoo on my beautiful bottom which was lovely and
passionate like a romantic love song.
The tattoo was of a pair of red high heels which really looked great!
Say what you want about my dinky lover, he never treated me
                                                    second rate.
And when I wanted my belly button pierced, he paid for this
and a diamond and gold chain too.
I don't want to hurt him by not wearing stilettos as most girls do!
But my feet really ache and ache, I'm in such a state.
Oh why, oh why does my lover need to see me always as his shoe mate?
I'll dress for him in ultra mini minis that almost show my bum too!
Cut slinky and low, showing my bare belly button and swinging
diamond and chain on daring and proud view.

But oh how I wish I could cure my aching feet!
My plates of meat which my chiropodist says I should keep out of
the heat.
Still my lover makes me laugh as I've never laughed before;
And if that means I still have to suffer in six inch stilettos;
Then I guess I'll just have to walk more slowly through life's six inch
stillettos walking and teetering grand tour!

Jackie J Docherty

MY LOVE

I have loved and I have lost,
How my heart breaks and at what cost,
I gave my love so totally
And all he did was take from me.

He took my love, he took my heart,
I was not perfect for my part,
But how I loved and how I yearned
And yet he took, my love he spurned.

He took my joy, he took my pride,
He drove my confidence inside,
He made me feel without worth,
He made me feel less than the earth.

It seems he wanted to control
My life, my thoughts, my very soul.
But came the time I must rebel
Or ever be within this hell.

He had yet one more stroke to play
To bring me back along his way,
He threatened, bullied, terrified
But still, though close, I just survived.

No matter how I loved this man,
He had no infinite right to plan
To overpower my life's freewill
Nor contemplate, with drink to kill.

To take my life was not his right,
To use the drink to give him might
Was just the coward's way to deal
With me, because I would not come to heel.

I lost my love for evermore,
And as my tears drop to the floor
I know even if I could forgive
The act, next time I would not live.

Marie Jay

DON'T GO

I'll never understand the truth
your love has gone but where's the proof.
To me our lives go hand in hand
and on our feet we always land.

So this is it, you've had enough
you say goodbye and pack your stuff.

Yes go and leave, I'll be okay
this life alone, now on your way.

It hurts, I'm mad, confused and stuck
I've missed the plot, I'm out of luck.

It's gone, my life walked out the door
so many years, what were they for?

I'll phone our friends, I need a drink
she will come back, I've time to think.

Who needs a woman any how -
she nags and moans, the stupid cow.

The beer's worn off with my poor head
I miss her love when all is said.

I know I'm wrong but in the end
I wish I hadn't sh***ed her friend.

James L Wood

ON THIS HER BIRTHDAY

Memories flood back evoking our yesterdays
Of youth when carefree and so in love.
What is this word love?
This heartache, this pounding
This pining.
She now, so far away, in another's arms.
So far away on this her day.

Memories flood back that fill with joy and pain
Yet show no mercy to my feelings
Such as they are
My soul laid bare
Life so unfair and, yes I bloody care.

My soul, a winter wasteland
Stripped by a frost, so harsh that all is sterile
As memories of lost love
Echo in the sadness of my mind
On this her birthday.

Maddoc Martin

LIKE TORTURE

In you I trusted implicitly
Not an easy thing for me
Now not the slightest affection shown
More time for 'those' you haven't known
Call me fickle or maybe foolish
Not even one kiss from lips I miss
Now left both sad and sickened
My heart so strong . . . strickened
You live . . . you die
Your tears run dry
Like torture . . . my dear departed
I believed in every word she said!

Lynn Thompson

TORN

To try and fall
Out of love
When you know things
Aren't quite right,
Is twice as hard
As a coconut -
Hard to crack
And just out of reach!

Lyn Sandford

FOOLISH FOR LOVING YOU

So foolish a person for loving you
Thinking that you loved me too
Thinking it was a second chance in life
Oh to be loved, unconditionally, without strife

We had our good times, we had our bad
But too much drink, he really had
We married each other, for better or worse
But, the whisky he drank, became a curse

He did nothing, but abuse me, after the drink
Pushing my heard into the sink
Asking for forgiveness, the very next day
Feeling quite sorry for him, in a pathetic way

Forgiving him, time and time again
Although it caused so much pain
Till, one day he just had to depart
Oh, please be still, my foolish heart

A third chance came, as looking up above
To the great god of mercy, the great god of love
Who came into my heart, some years ago
Although I was two fools, for loving so

Jean P McGovern

I'M NOT READY

Hey babe, we've been together a little while
And now you wanna take me down the aisle,
You know you mean the world to me,
But I'm just not ready.

All your friends have tied the knot,
And some say that may be my lot.
What's the worry when we're going steady?
I can't explain, but I'm just not ready.

Splitting up may be the thing to do,
But I can't imagine my world without you.
The six years between us now, seems quite great,
As I still have lots to do before it's too late.

Can you give me a little time?
Perhaps leave me alone a little while?
I have answers to find and places to see,
I'm so sorry babe that I'm not ready.

Annabelle Lilly

THE BALLAD OF FRENCHIE LE PEW

Of all the girls that I once knew
None compare to Frenchie Le Pew
No one spoke when she appeared
She was the one most men feared.

With eyes of ice and lips like fire
She was the object of desire
To say it right and give her due
None could match Frenchie Le Pew.

Now men lust and yearn to see
The finest woman yet to be
But they would gladly form a queue
To see the lovely Miss Le Pew

A body made from mans' desire
To look and want and never tire
Of seeing paradise in motion
That magic urge, that secret potion.

Upon my tombstone let it say
That next to her I long to lay
And let me mention once to you
I'll always love Frenchie Le Pew.

John Mitchell

THINKING OF YOU

I wonder if it's a crime
To think about you all the time.
In the morning
Last thing at night.
In the dark
And in the light.

Is it just infatuation?
Or chemistry, a chain reaction
Not going anywhere,
Being with you without a care.
There's always been this attraction,
Can you feel it, just a fraction?

I wonder if it's a crime,
To freeze this moment,
Stop the time.
Listening to our hearts beating fast
And wishing we could always last.

Annette K Aiken

PASSION OF ONE

Without passion in my life, I began to suffer
plodding on times path from one place to another
For too many years I have been kept
in life's hand, death bag which I no longer accept
A mere existence from beginning to end
until buried in passion, my life I did lend
My heart pounded thunder, my lips ran dry
my soul wreaked tragedy that condemned me to cry
A once hollow mind without true thought
teaches the man within, who could not be taught
Rain clouds above will not darken my way
I have regained my passion this very day
Mere words on paper is where I begin
but the warmth and fulfilment comes from within
The passion inspires me, my life is on fire
my mind is filled with thoughts of desire
Never retire when there's much to be done
stand up and be counted it all starts with one
One single thought one seed to be planted
a single word yes! And our dreams are granted

C D Spooner

LOVE

*L*ilies and roses
Are flowers of love
Which exactly like you
Fell from Heaven above

*O*ver rooftops, through rainclouds
I still find your face
With your shiny, bright eyes
And no hair out of place

*V*ivid memories of you
Keep on flooding back
You are beauty, you are
My aphrodisiac

*E*arth's a wonderful place now
And I just must let you
Know that now that you're in it
I'll never forget you

Kevin McNulty

LET LOVE GUIDE YOU THROUGH

When all fails and you have nowhere to turn
Let love guide you through

When there's no one to turn to
No one to dry your tears or comfort you
Let love guide you through

When the burden gets heavy
And no one seems to understand
No one's there to hold your hand
Be strong; and let love guide you through

God is love; and
Love is all you need to see you through

Janice Simone Ramkissoon

A LIFE OF LOVE

My love in life, my love in death,
My love in play, my love in rest
You're my love in everything I do
I could never express how much I love you.
The first time I saw your sparkling eyes
My feelings took me by surprise
I'd never felt this kind of emotion
My world started spinning round in slow motion.
I never want to see us part
That really would just break my heart.
I love your face, your laugh and smile
I have to be with you even for a while
I love your sense of humour and personality
I can't believe you're in reality.
You and me are just a perfect match
You really are a dreamy catch!
I still can't believe how lucky I am
I go all giddy when I hold your hand.
Together we can get through anything
Comfort or pain, thick or thin.
We're always there to help each other
I really don't want any other.
I love the time I spend with you
I cherish memories as if they're new.
We've got so much to look forward to as we grow
In the future our love will really show.
I look forward to what we have to come
But for now I'll enjoy our time together whilst we're young
So just in case you didn't know! I'll tell you one more time
I really truly love you and am so lucky you're mine.

Karen Stacey (16)

THE KEY TO MY HEART

The key to my heart
Is what you hold,
You make me happy
You are my life.

The key to my heart
Is what you hold,
The first time I saw you
I knew you were the one.

The key to my heart
Is what you hold,
When we kiss
My legs turn to jelly.

The key to my heart
Is what you hold,
You're the one I dream of
You're the one I run too.

The key to my heart
Is what you hold,
I will never let you go
As you mean everything to me.

The key to my heart
Is what you hold,
Words cannot tell you
Just how much I love you.

Catrina Lawrence

THE COMPLIMENT

'Hello darlin' nice one luv!' came a yell from the panda car as
it slowed at Sutton's traffic lights, bored coppers looking for
someone to nick - wrong place Sutton, all squeaky clean suburbia.
Neighbourhood Watch, Nonsuch Park, old eccentrics,
walking the dog. Trees and trees, well rounded cats
all seeing green-eyed through neatly trimmed
luxuriant hedged gardens.

'Not from where I'm standing' said my one-time boyfriend
in a booming voice. People at the bus stop shuffled in their
embarrassment, looked at pavements, checked watches;
some sidelong glances shot our way.

Hurt, I fell silent, a tear welled up but was suppressed,
my face flushed up with anger, tiny needle sensations spread
across it momentarily.
The unprovoked attack was like a punch in the stomach,
below the belt as my friend later aptly remarked.
How could this man I'd known for two years love me
as he claimed, I thought.
When I found a story done for his writing class, scribbled
on a discarded piece of paper about how much he hated my
glutinous hair and other malicious jibes, I realised he didn't!

Some months later in a frenzied attack, he tore the clothes
from my back and huge clumps of my blonde hair out
saying, 'I told you I didn't like that style.'

Gemma Davies

MY DREAM

As I close my eyes and drift off into a deep sleep
Visions of you immediately appear and invade my dreams
A feeling of comfort and love takes over me
A film fest of our future begins to play freely
I smile in my sleep as a result of what I see
A walk through the park holding hands with my Najee
Whispers of true love is heard through the trees
Hundreds of cherry blossoms dancing to the breeze
A moment to pause as he holds me tight
As he briefly looks into my eyes
You are my life, my love; you're everything to me
Always with you is where I prefer to be
Tears of joy rapidly make its way to accompany me
Because of the words spoken by my Najee
He sits upon the grass his back against the tree
Gently I lay upon his chest as he embraces me
I began to speak now it's my turn
To express my feelings for him through my words
You've changed my world and made me as happy as can be
There's no place I'd rather be
Our love for one another is unique, one of a kind
Has to be the intervention of the devine
He bends his head with the intention to kiss
His pillow soft lips. I dare not miss
My world is complete girl, because of you
No one else in this world will ever do
I awake with a smile on my face
Oh my god. I excitingly say
A dream like this is surely from you
My god, I pray that dreams do come true.

Tonya Barber

THE ONE

I want mine to be the touch you need
Before you sleep at night
I want my arms to be the ones
The ones to hold you tight!

I want to be the one who's there
To wipe away your tears
I want to be the one you need
To protect you from your fears.

I want mine to be the face you see
Whenever you close your eyes
I want our love to be the one
The one that never dies!

Colin Morrow

LOVE

Love is a very strong emotion,
can make you smile
or cry like an ocean,
when times are hard
you need someone there,
to show you some love
and that they care,
love can bring you closer together
to fight through life
whatever the weather,
with more love in the world
and people who care,
life would be better and easier to bare.

Rachael Ford

A DREAM OF LOVE

There he stood before me,
his eyes blended amongst the trees of the forests,
Was he a shadow that appeared in my dream?
How real did this seem?

The forgotten tomorrow's,
but my time was borrowed.
For a moment this was real,
if only you knew how I feel.

In my dream, I was in love,
but in reality I was only a dove.
I fly with the wind,
for I know I have never sinned.

Maggie Hickinbotham

REMEMBER

Remember me when I have gone away,
Think of me at least once a day.
Remember the small laughs that we shared
And how much I cared.
Remember my face,
Remember my smile
As you may not see it for a while.
Remember all the memories that you hold
For they are far more precious than gold.

Nicky Stecker

OH, MY GOSH! OH, MY GOSH! OH, MY GOSH!
(A poem about a girl called Jennifer!)

Oh, my! That kiss! And just for me!
How cute, how sweet, how quaint!
I'm kinda lost . . . pure ecstasy!
I hope that I don't faint!
Oh, gosh! One more! Upon my lips!
Must be my lucky day!
Oh, wow! A third! My heartbeat dips -
It almost slipped away!
Please stop! No more! Oh, not again!
Four times? Don't make it five!
I'm not as strong as other men!
I don't think I'd survive!
Good gracious, girl! I'm not that cute!
Five kisses in a row?
I think it's time for you to scoot!
One kiss before you go?
Did I kiss back? Confession time!
Jennifer! Je t'adore!
Exquisite kisses, so sublime!
Addicted now for sure!
Now I see why! It's kinda nice!
It's awesome, don't you think?
It kinda takes you by surprise
To find two hearts in sync!
Why did we wait so long, my dear?
Why were we so reserved?
Thank god, at last we've lost our fear
And got what we deserved!
Such tenderness! Such happiness!
Such are the joys of life!
I've got to ask you now I guess . . .
Erm . . . will . . . you . . . be . . . my . . . wife?

Denis Martindale

WHAT IS LOVE?

Love tells us to be silent
when words wound someone's heart.
Love is patient and forgiving
if a quarrel someone starts.

Love is thoughtfulness for others,
when the winds of change do blow.
Love is deaf to scandal-mongering,
when the tales begin to flow.

Love is always being ready
when someone in need may call.
Love is finding strength to help them
'tis the greatest love of all.

Love is *real*, when you've forgiven
- someone, who has caused you pain.
How many times must we forgive them?
Seventy times and then again.

Monica C Gibson

In Time

I don't know what's going on?
I can't feel a single touch.
But I feel my heart beating hard,
Maybe I love you too much.
I feel my eyes getting tired,
It's happening every day.
I can't see as far as I used to,
As you're standing in the way.

I try to peer around you,
To see where I am going.
I can't seem to focus,
The wind keeps blowing and blowing.
Most of the time the weather is bad,
The rain just falls and falls.
A feeling like I have nowhere to go,
Trapped within four walls.

I know one day I'll be able to break free,
And find a person to trust, care for and believe in me.

Natalie Ellis

THREE WORDS

The winter snow's
Crisp beneath my feet.
The man I love passes
But we dare not speak.
I hang my head
But not with shame,
For empty words spoken
Have nothing to gain.
I can feel his eyes,
As they tear at my heart.
But in his life,
I have no place, no right, no part.
People move around me,
Though I feel so still.
Tears find their home
As my eyes start to fill.
The cold winds bite with bitter force,
An anger felt with compassion.
Only to be snatched by remorse,
His breath I can touch,
As his stare grows deeper.
My heart beats faster,
Begging to be unlocked by its keeper.
I dare not look back,
Or try and lift my head.
This pain I cannot endure,
From the promises once said.
Inside I bleed as he twists the knife,
When he whispers, 'I love you,'
His three words not for me,
These words for his wife.

Andrea Benita Ross

LOVE'S FEAR

I've braved the Atlantic's tempest,
I've cast the Hippogriff down,
Slaying serpents at the wind's behest,
I've stolen Jupiter's crown;
I've swam with Krakens in deep, blue sea,
I've stood at the epicentre's quake,
But now I'm nearing love's vicinity
My fragile limbs, they start to shake.

I've completed many a noble quest,
I've given the poor their gold,
I've sailed round isles more blessed,
I've relaxed the tax man's hold;
I've immersed myself in ice and fire
I've descended from the clouds above -
Now why does my brave spirit retire,
When confronted by this upstart, love?

Heys Stuart Wolfenden

MOTHER-IN-LAW

I have a mother-in-law's plant
Given as a gift to me
Often I give her a cup of tea
She sits in the corner
As good as gold
Spiky green, marked leaves
Now she is sprouting little shoots

Surrounded by spider plant and an angel trumpet
No wonder her son fancied me as his bit of crumpet.

Christine M Wicks

JUST THE SAME OLD ME

Yes, it's here again 'Valentine's Day'
I guess, thinking, and drifting away
Now I realise so far the cards amount to
A total of 52, just from
The man I married who, although
Doesn't know how,
Each day I awake, I shake
With pain, you cannot see it
But it's there all the time.
Try to conceal how ill I feel
Pretending I am normal and it's not real
Try as I may, it won't go away
Yes, it's here with me, day after day
But so are you, that's okay
So inside I am happy
Still the same old me
So as long as you are with me
I will always say, I am happy to be
The mother to Carol, so bright and gay
And you still will be my Valentine, today.

B Clark

LOVE AT FIRST SIGHT

It was on the terrace
When I first saw her standing there
Moonlight shining on her golden hair
All that I could do was stare
Her silhouette made my heart race
Although I could not see her face
Slowly she turned around and smiled
It was then that I became beguiled
Then she took me by surprise
The look of love was in her eyes
I now believe that it is right
There's such a thing as love at first sight.

D L Critchley

SAFE IN MY HEART

(In loving memory of Glenn W Isaaks
1962 - 2002 RIP)

So now you're gone,
You're at peace,
A smile on your face,
You're finally happy

I'll miss you dear,
You're always here,
Safe in my heart.

You were so loved
By all you knew,
And I want to say,
'Thanks for the memories.'

I'll miss you dear,
You're always here,
Safe in my heart.

Though calm by nature,
You were fighting to the end.
I'll always love you
Like a father,
My dear friend.

I'll miss you dear,
You're always here,
Safe in my heart.

Stephen Howsam

COURTSHIP

'Would you give me your last Rollo?'
To my boyfriend I once said.
He replied and said he wouldn't
Then he told me to drop dead
'Would you climb the highest mountain,
Swim a shark infested sea
Dive into a burning building
Do you think - to rescue me?'
'I have better things to do now,'
Was all he had to say
So I slapped him in the kisser
Then I quickly ran away
Well . . . I told him he was ugly
Had a face just like a flook
He replied that I was ugly too
No page three, in a book
When I asked him if he would die for me
'To that,' he said, 'no fear
You can die all by yourself, you can
Just don't involve me dear.'
Well . . . we always argued rings around
About every little thing
For we were quite the opposites
Him a Woolworth's vase, me Ming
Three months into our courtship
He asked to marry me
I just refused the offer
I was far too young, you see
Me being all of fourteen years
Him being just fifteen
He said he didn't mean it and quickly left the scene
Now that was quite some years ago
Before we both got wed
Now if he ever argues
I lock him in his shed

We have got two lovely children
Maybe a third is on the way
Do I still love him?
Sometimes I do, but sadly not today!

Eleanor Dunn

WITHIN

Here I am searching
Deep down in my mind,
Desperate to discover
What I need to find.
As I travel deeper
I cannot understand
Why the darkness
Gathers all around.
Swiftly I'm beginning
To give up on hope
Tears are now falling,
I really cannot cope.
Then just as I'm failing
A soft spot I feel,
There is hope after all
Cannot believe it's real.
Slowly it's emerging
The gentleness and love
That can be found within you
A gift from Heaven above.

E M Gough

COMFORT IN COTTON SHEETS

In this world of cotton sheets
and nights of star-less skies,
there is comfort from the dark
in very short supply.
So if I ask to take your hand
to guide your heart to mine,
perhaps you'll see the wisdom
of a moment caught in time.
And if I ask to dance with you,
just hold me close and sway.
I will lead you through the steps
and help you find the way.
So look into my soulful eyes
and journey to the ledge,
take the path that fades away
till you're standing at the edge.
And when you gaze upon the view,
you'll see what's really there.
Then I'll ask if you could stay,
in this house of disrepair.
And if you choose to stand with me,
those cotton sheets will warm.
The stars will shine again for us
when comfort is reborn.

M M Graham

TAINTED LOVE

He told me he loved me when he tried to get me in his bed,
but when I ask for commitment, he says I'm messing with his head.
When the football's on he forgets I'm even there,
he makes me get his beers as he can't possibly leave his chair.
He always leaves the seat up and the lid off the shampoo,
he squeezes toothpaste from the top and is on the brink of death
                                          when he catches flu.
If I ask him to do the washing he says he's got a phobia of stains,
and if I make him do the ironing he passes out with fake stomach pains.
Well I guess this is how it goes with love at first sight,
but I'll tell you what - next time I'm gonna put up a better fight.

Nicola Pitchers

MY HEART

First you get the strings,
And play your loving tune.
Then my heart it sings.
And swells like a balloon.
It starts to build up pace,
And beat for all it's worth.
Then I lose all sense of place,
And doubt I'm of this Earth.
Oh high above the clouds,
Beyond our atmosphere.
Away from all my earthly shrouds,
So far the moon seems near.
You know you hold my heart
Upon your breath, I hang,
And if we ever part
My heart would just go bang.

Sid 'de' Knees